Richard Strauss
Der Rosenkavalier Waltz

Transcribed for Violin and Piano
by Richard Walters

DISTRIBUTED BY

7777 W. BLUEMOUND RD. P.O. BOX 13819 MILWAUKEE, WI 53213

www.boosey.com
www.halleonard.com

Der Rosenkavalier Waltz

Der Rosenkavalier
(The Rose Bearer)

opera in three acts

music by Richard Strauss
libretto by Hugo von Hofmannsthal

Composed 1909–1910. First performed in Dresden, Germany, at the Court Opera, 26 January 1911.

This waltz, as adapted for violin and piano, is from the end of Act 2 of the opera, which takes place in mid-18th century Vienna. The scene is of the buffoon Baron Ochs, who has just been barely wounded in a scuffle over his affections for a woman much too young for him. He sips wine as he recovers, left alone, and receives a note from "Mariandel," actually the young Octavian in disguise, who aims to foil the Baron's romantic plans. As Ochs becomes tipsy with happy hope over the prospect of meeting "Mariandel," the music lilts into the famous waltz. With an opera set in Vienna, the great Strauss could not resist composing a piece in honor of that city's favorite dance music, although its use in *Der Rosenkavalier* is anachronistic, since the distinctive style of the Viennese waltz did not evolve until the 19th century, taken to its zenith by Johann Strauss, Jr.

The composer adapted a Waltz Sequence (no. 1), from Acts 1–2, from *Der Rosenkavalier* for orchestra in 1925. Strauss adapted the Waltz Sequence (no. 2), from Act 3, from *Der Rosenkavalier* for orchestra in 1934.

Der Rosenkavalier Waltz

Der Rosenkavalier-Walzer

RICHARD STRAUSS
(1864–1949)
Transcribed for violin and piano by Richard Walters

Walzertempo, sehr gemächlich beginnend ($\dot{\ } = 48$)
(*Tempo di valse, assai comodo da prima*)
(*Waltz time, very leisurely at first*)

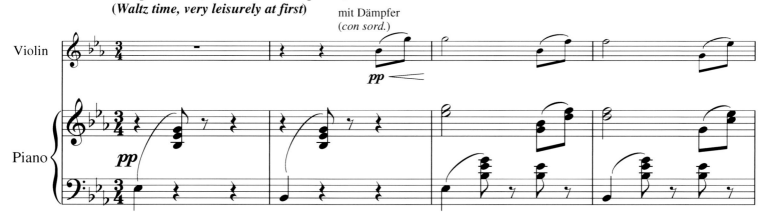

Violin

Richard Strauss
Der Rosenkavalier Waltz

Transcribed for Violin and Piano
by Richard Walters

BOOSEY & HAWKES

DISTRIBUTED BY

7777 W. BLUEMOUND RD. P.O. BOX 13819 MILWAUKEE, WI 53213

www.boosey.com
www.halleonard.com

Der Rosenkavalier Waltz

Der Rosenkavalier
(The Rose Bearer)

opera in three acts

music by Richard Strauss
libretto by Hugo von Hofmannsthal

Composed 1909–1910. First performed in Dresden, Germany, at the Court Opera, 26 January 1911.

This waltz, as adapted for violin and piano, is from the end of Act 2 of the opera, which takes place in mid-18th century Vienna. The scene is of the buffoon Baron Ochs, who has just been barely wounded in a scuffle over his affections for a woman much too young for him. He sips wine as he recovers, left alone, and receives a note from "Mariandel," actually the young Octavian in disguise, who aims to foil the Baron's romantic plans. As Ochs becomes tipsy with happy hope over the prospect of meeting "Mariandel," the music lilts into the famous waltz. With an opera set in Vienna, the great Strauss could not resist composing a piece in honor of that city's favorite dance music, although its use in *Der Rosenkavalier* is anachronistic, since the distinctive style of the Viennese waltz did not evolve until the 19th century, taken to its zenith by Johann Strauss, Jr.

The composer adapted a Waltz Sequence (no. 1), from Acts 1–2, from *Der Rosenkavalier* for orchestra in 1925. Strauss adapted the Waltz Sequence (no. 2), from Act 3, from *Der Rosenkavalier* for orchestra in 1934.

Der Rosenkavalier Waltz

Der Rosenkavalier-Walzer

RICHARD STRAUSS
(1864–1949)

Violin

Transcribed for violin and piano by Richard Walters

Walzertempo, sehr gemächlich beginnend ($\downarrow$. = 48)
(*Tempo di valse, assai comodo da prima*)
(*Waltz time, very leisurely at first*)
mit Dämpfer
(*con sord.*)

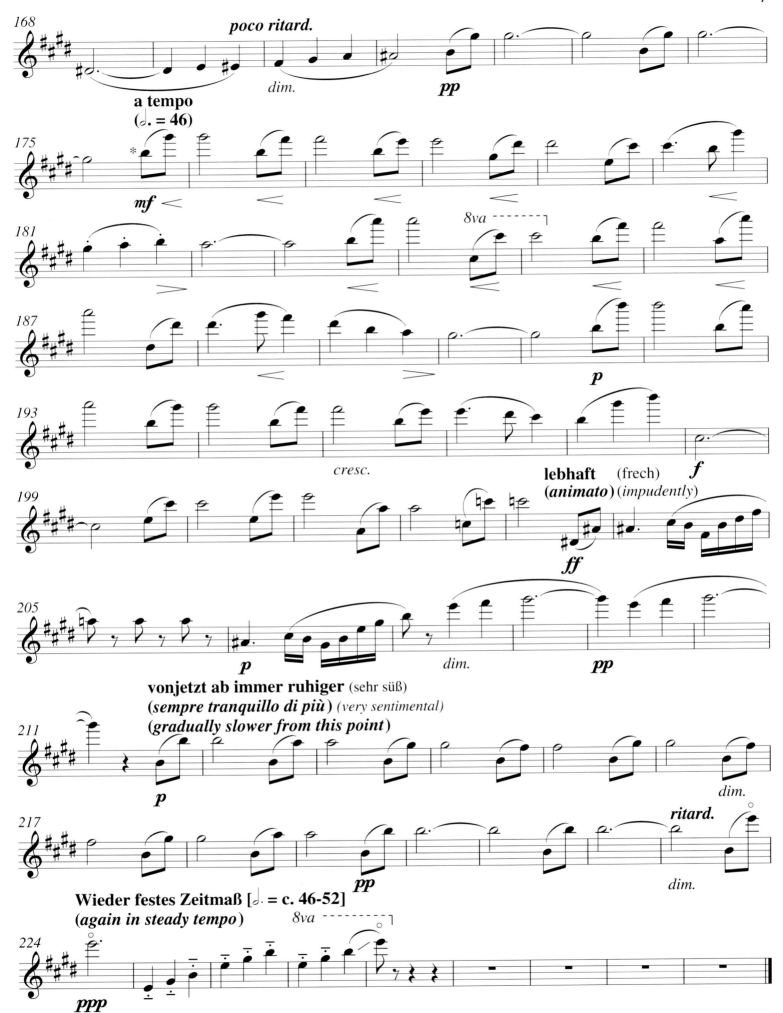

* Anmerkung aus der Partitur: Die Auftakte in den Streichern stets in dem süßlichen Wiener glissando.
Note in the orchestral score: The strings to play throughout on the up-beat with sugary Viennese glissando.

* Anmerkung aus der Partitur: Die Auftakte in den Streichern stets in dem süßlichen Wiener glissando.
Note in the orchestral score: The strings to play throughout on the up-beat with sugary Viennese glissando.